ANNI SENN

KARMA-FREE
in the New Time

good adventures publishing

KARMA-FREE IN THE NEW TIME

©2015, Anni Sennov and Good Adventures Publishing
First edition, first impression
Set with Cambria
Layout: Anni Sennov – www.sennovpartners.com
Cover design: Michael Bernth – www.monovoce.dk
Cover photo: Semko Belcerski - www.semko.dk
Author photo: Lisbeth Hjort – www.lisbethhjort.dk

Original title in Danish:
"Karma-fri i den nye tid"
Translated into English by: Lotte and David Young
Proofread and adapted by: Sue Jonas Dupuis

ISBN 978-87-92549-64-8

CONTENTS

PROLOGUE

When this book was originally published in Denmark in 1997, it caused a great furore in spiritual circles. Who did I think I was as a healer and clairvoyant to declare that soul energy here on Earth was now definitively over? How could I say that all children from the mid–1990s were born with only spirit energy in their auras, while other writers still referred to soul energy as the ultimate energy state of human consciousness? Who on Earth (or elsewhere) was my spiritual source of information?

Was it Sananda, Archangel Michael, Sanat Kumara or the Virgin Mary, although, of course, none of these spiritual beings would supposedly have come out with such a load of old nonsense?

In reply, I can only say that as far as I understood it myself at that time, I was in contact with Source itself and not one of its channels, since I was someone who was considered to be a pure channel for the supreme energy myself. However, I would never have said that to anyone in the late 1990s, because I was, of course, not physically capable of walking on water, unlike certain ancient oracles.

Now, in 2015, the support for my message about the influx of pure spirit energy to planet Earth has become increasingly strong – especially in Scandinavia – which makes me very happy. It is therefore relevant to reprint this book in a new, updated edition.

I hope you will find great joy and understanding from reading this book, updated at a time when Planet Earth is about to move into even higher and faster levels of frequency.

Happy reading!

Anni Sennov
January 2015

THE BOOK – IN BRIEF

Since this book is relatively easy to read but may be difficult to absorb on a consciousness and comprehension level, I have chosen to start with a short, compact version of its entire contents, so that the general outline will be fairly clear to the reader from the start.

****

Up until recent times, Earth's spiritual hinterland was governed exclusively by a Hierarchy, which consisted of two types of energy, namely, the Great White Brotherhood and the Dark Brotherhood who worked together. However, they cannot claim to have done a particularly good job, especially regarding the earthly plane.

On Earth, these two spiritual methods of governance most often worked against each other. The Great White Brotherhood was always perceived by most spiritual people as the place where the 'good' helpers came from, whilst the Dark Brotherhood represented the shadow side, or 'evil'. However, things were really not like that at all but human consciousness was simply not capable of understanding this on an everyday consciousness level up until now. At this moment in time, all children are born with a new spiritual structure within them which is completely free of soul energy.

The spiritual Hierarchy in the hinterland of Earth's consciousness was always structured like a pyramid, with less conscious souls at the bottom and a few spiritually conscious ones at the top. This pyramid structure became too limited and constricting over time for some of the highly evolved people who inhabited Planet Earth at that time. Many of these people, who had done a tremendous job over the years for the spiritual hinterland, had not always felt well rewarded for their exceptional efforts for the Whole. It is just not enough just to get your reward in heaven, it being impossible to pay your bills with 'pure' spiritual energy. Also some spiritually inspired people had always felt that the concept of karma, where you reap what you have previously sown, was not relevant to their own lives.

Over the last 30 years and as an alternative to the old Hierarchy, a new and even more powerful spiritual source, with increased manifestation potential, has been opening up. The energy of this source is infinite and by virtue of its lack of structure, gives full freedom of movement and direction for all the souls who wish to move into pure spirit energy, regarding any aspect of their physical and spiritual lives and development here on Planet Earth.

The new source/entity contains all the polarities within itself - light and dark, male and female, as well as high and low energy combined and thus it offers each individual every opportunity to choose to take either the 'light' road or the 'dark' road, or even both – whatever is best for Earth, although this may sound completely crazy to many people's ears.

The new spiritual entity, called the *Shamballah force*, is an energy that we have always been aware of here on Earth under the name of the *Power of Divine Will*. However, up until now, this energy was perceived as being totally unattainable for all earthly souls, which, in a way, it was. The fact is, that in order to be connected To that energy with your everyday consciousness, it is a precondition that your aura consists of exclusively pure spirit energy. Today, this is possible through AuraTransformation™. During an AuraTransformation™, human consciousness moves from soul consciousness, which belongs to the three lower energy bodies in the aura – the etheric body, the astral body and the lower mental body – to connect instead with pure spirit energy in the form of the higher mental body. This energy moves closer and closer to the physical body with the new balance body as a communication link between body and spirit.

So far, it has only been possible for masters and archangels to have access to this energy, since they, with their highly spiritual consciousness, were always at the top of the Hierarchy. Now though, the level of consciousness of many people on Earth has grown to such an extent that they can, gradually and with every-day consciousness, accommodate the idea of actually having a much greater energy potential than any spiritually inclined people had previously thought possible.

A great many people with master, archangel and solar angel energy have in fact incarnated on the planet at this time and it is now their turn to take over the Hierarchy's energy obligations in relation to Planet Earth. They will, however, do this in a more earthly- oriented manner, as they truly are matter (i.e. human), as this is what is needed for the establishing of the new energy on Earth.

The Shamballah energy is the power centre of all the masters, archangels and solar angels and with its combination of all types of energy in one and the same pool, it has a truly enormous mani-festation and materialisation power on the earthly plane, based on all the ideas that people send out on the everyday conscious-ness plane here on Earth. This is a manifestation and materiali-sation capacity which people can learn to master in their daily lives if they choose to have an AuraTransformation™.

The energy of the New Time that many people refer to today as being tomorrow's supreme energy comes, quite simply, from the Shamballah force. Moreover, the energy of the New Time corresponds to the channelling energy with which many spiri-tually aware people have been in contact over the years, through their connection with various spiritual guides at the top of the Hierarchy.

So far, it is only the masters and archangels in Earth's spiritual hinterland who have had direct access to the Shamballah force. Today, people here on Planet Earth will be able to have their heads right up in heaven – if they so choose – and they can also choose to become conscious guides for themselves and for those closest to them by using their intuition. This means, that in the future, many oracles will be unemployed!

The integration of the energy of the New Time can happen through an AuraTransformation™ carried out by an authorised Aura Mediator™, who has, of course had an AuraTransformation™ him/herself and who, in addition, has a large capacity and total balance in their consciousness. This makes it possible for them to be able to have a comprehensive view of the client's full spiritual consciousness as it unfolds completely during the AuraTransformation™ process.

The purpose of the AuraTransformation™ is that you upgrade the three lower energy bodies in the aura, which are replaced by a new magnetic and powerfully protective energy body – the balance body – the structure of which is entirely consistent with the magic Shamballah force's basic energy and its current energy influx on Earth.

During an AuraTransformation™, people relinquish any karma and thus become capable of working consciously with the energy of the New Time in their daily lives. This also means that their auras will not get burnt away because of the very high energy frequencies now coming through to Earth from the invisible spiritual hinterland.

At this point in time, many people are living without the protection of a soul aura but they are unaware of this. They no longer have an aura either because they have been exposed to shock and unpleasant experiences or even major allergic influences from their surroundings, the food they eat, or quite simply because they have been working with pure light with healing and meditation for several years. These people benefit greatly from an AuraTransformation™ so that their personal energy can be upgraded in accordance with the new energy influx

Just by the way, it is important to understand that nowadays you are not going to die from walking around without the three lower energy bodies in your aura if you have the energy capacity to operate within the pure spirit energy framework. On the other hand, you may have been feeling invisible and overlooked if you are surrounded by people who are not as spiritually conscious as yourself.

It is not enough in itself that people, due to the integration of the new aura, acquire the will and the power to be able to get a whole lot done. Your motivation and will should preferably be used for something constructive on Planet Earth. In this context, the overall spiritual goal of the Whole is to achieve balance. Everyone, regardless of their nature and energy, is born on this Earth with the sole purpose of helping to create balance and we all do this at some level in our lives.

That fact that people have the new balance body integrated into their aura during an AuraTransformation™ is not enough in itself to create a balance in their personal lives. After the AuraTransformation™, a balancing of the masculine and feminine energies in the aura is carried out to maintain the new balanced state in the aura and in some people's cases, it may be necessary to have one or even several subsequent balancings.

PLANET EARTH'S SPIRITUAL STRUCTURE

THE HIERARCHY

All the planets in our solar system are different from each other in their structure and the overall purpose of the respective planets' existences and the function of the planets' structures – be it their earthly, physical or spiritual structure etc. – can vary infinitely, even if two planets, purely from an energy point of view, can appear to be very similar to each other.

All humans here on Planet Earth are also different from one another in their energy structures, even though most of us are born with identical energy bodies in the aura.

Up until this millennium, the population of Earth had drawn its spiritual guidance from the Hierarchy, where most people preferred to consult the Great White Brotherhood. The other party in the Earth's spiritual hinterland – the Dark Brotherhood – equated with the shadow side of human beings, was completely ignored by most people working with and developing personal consciousness.

However, the Light and Dark Brotherhoods have always worked consciously together, even though we humans have not been able to perceive it as such but we have to understand that this state of affairs is perfectly logical, as the integration of balance has to start somewhere!

As mentioned previously, the Hierarchy was like a pyramid with many souls on the bottom, representing heaviness, spiritual ignorance and bodily strength. These souls did not have particularly potent manifestation powers since they have lacked the knowledge and comprehension regarding what they should actually be trying to manifest in their earthly lives.

On the other hand, the top of the Hierarchy was represented by spiritual energies in a very pure form that had their source in *God*. This represented the highest source of energy that we as humans were able to draw energy from.

Furthermore, the top of the pyramid consisted of the spirit energy mass and auras of different masters and archangels. It is to these spiritual forces that all the souls on the bottom of the pyramid were sending thoughts and prayers when something was needed or lacking in their lives.

The foundation stones of the pyramid can be seen to represent *obedience to authority*, meaning that less evolved souls were obedient to those with greater knowledge or higher frequency and also *karma*, where all souls, through their thoughts and actions, constantly needed to make themselves worthy of gaining greater spiritual insight as well as a higher energy frequency. Then they would be able to have access to a higher level in the Hierarchy.

Although the structure of the Hierarchy may have appeared to provide a lot of security for the community, it did not leave much room for those of natural ability to flourish in the best way; at least, not until they had proved their competence.

THE TRANSITION TO THE NEW

Due to the intense energy work, over many years, of spiritual people on Earth, the level of consciousness on this planet has risen to the point where the New Time Shamballah energy has been able to slide right down into the lowest frequencies on Earth and therefore penetrate matter itself. The Hierarchy, with its highly differentiated energy structure (light and dark, high and low) has not kept pace with this expansion of consciousness.

Those with great consciousnesses in the Hierarchy have certainly not been able to penetrate into the consciousness of all people on Earth and to share the message that we need to cooperate with the many varied and strange energies that are out and about in order to help create an overall balance, for the good of the Whole. Furthermore, the Hierarchy has not been able to keep up with the gradually increasing consciousness demands that the conscious and spiritually aware section of the population has formulated.

People who, on a soul level, have been operating very high up in the Hierarchy have gradually become aware that pure, beautiful thoughts and meditation aren't enough on their own. It is also necessary to take action to accelerate development on Earth – we are not talking about technological development here but rather about general human development, where the aspiration is for an overall balance between the physical and the spiritual.

As Planet Earth was in the doldrums in terms of spiritual development for many years, it was a relatively manageable task for the Hierarchy to help we human beings. However, in the summer of 1996, our spiritual hinterland reached crisis point when energy frequencies increased rapidly on Earth, in a relatively short space of time.
The Hierarchy suddenly found that in some cases it had been

overtaken by the karma exemption which it had itself given to Earth's population back in 1987. Even though this was only nine years later, the exemption had already managed to exert influence the Whole.

Put simply, the karma exemption meant that it would only be necessary for a soul to settle 51% of its karma to finally ascend into the Light in the spiritual dimension and thus completely renounce any future incarnations in a physical body; a great many earthly souls had apparently already accepted this opportunity, which created great confusion on the spiritual plane.

In the summer of 1996, it suddenly became impossible to distinguish between light and dark in the Hierarchy. This was the case no matter how high up you were on a consciousness and frequency level. The higher you got, the more energy layers you passed though, the worse the frustration became regarding the overlapping energies of light and dark. Where was the pure energy state which many associated with the Light?

The Hierarchy had lost the sharp dichotomy between the Great White Brotherhood and the Dark Brotherhood; seen with human eyes, it could very easily have looked as if many of the conscious Light workers here on Earth, who were able to pick up on this spiritual confusion, had suddenly given themselves permission to allow the Dark into their auras. Luckily, however, that is not what happened!

Inside the Hierarchy, there was full awareness of the confusion but as a totally spiritual dimension, it had no physical manifestation power in the earthly sphere and so was unable to spread the message about the new energy states. How then, was it going to get all the Light workers down here to understand that there were new spiritual ground rules on the way? Especially as not all spiritual people were clairvoyant and able to intercept or comprehend the new impulses from above.

It was therefore necessary to make certain strong Light people on Earth so aware of the state of affairs and in the shortest possible time, that the immediate confusion would be able to dissipate very quickly. Earth would then be able to move even higher up in frequency, which was necessary for its continued development.

The desire in the spiritual dimension and in the Hierarchy for any changes regarding raising the energy frequency, had to come from the physical dimension on Earth, which has the power of manifestation within it. The inspiration for the changes, on the other hand, was transmitted intuitively via spirit energy from the spiritual dimension to the physical, so that people who were very sensitive could intercept the signals from the Hierarchy and then manifest the desired change on the spiritual plane through the thoughts they were sending out from the physical plane here on Planet Earth.

The truth is that we humans have enormous power to influence global development, both spiritually and physically. What would have happened, for example, if we were to fail to respond to those spiritual impulses? Could we, if the occasion were to arise, help to delay development, or would our spiritual hinterland just find some other people to carry out the task if we were unwilling to make the effort? That is something worth thinking about...

One thing is certain: as people, we will never expand consciousness further than what is bearable and possible in the context of our daily lives. Should the spiritual dimension ask us to take on a very large task energy-wise and we feel unequal to the task, it is probably best to say no and to suggest that the task be transferred to other evolved people here on Earth who feel ready to contribute.

In the summer of 1996, the problems within the Hierarchy were due to so many souls moving very quickly because of karma exemption. This had happened because, amongst other things, these souls had behaved 'correctly' and because they had done exactly what was expected of them in specific circumstances. However, their ascension happened, in many cases, much too hastily, since many of them didn't really possess an energy capacity equal to the frequency in which they ended up finding themselves.

On closer inspection, it was possible, unbelievable though it may sound, to determine residues of darkness in the auras of several of the highest ranked masters and archangels in the Great White Brotherhood, as well as residues of light in the auras of high-ranking masters and archangels in the Dark Brotherhood. In the light of such confusion, who was really who?

A sort of grey area had also come into existence between the Light and Dark dimensions, which consisted of souls who could not work out which side to choose. This was a situation that did not serve Planet Earth, as it is the planet of development in our solar system and is therefore strongly dependent on receiving pure spiritual guidance from the higher powers.

The highest and purest light frequencies in our planet's spiritual hinterland could therefore no longer protect the most sensitive and intuitive part of Earth's population from receiving information of a contradictory nature from, amongst others, souls in the spiritual grey area. It is also true that throughout the ages, there have been very few Light workers on Earth who have allowed themselves to question the information they have received from the Light dimension and who have been evolved enough to assess whether they have received channelling directly from the Light dimension or not.

This inability to question the authenticity of information was, of course due, amongst other things, to the Hierarchy's original structure having been based on humility and obedience to authority of souls that were supposed to have greater knowledge and spiritual capacity than oneself. The energy at the top of the Hierarchy had always been perceived as being 'unique' and not many physically incarnated souls had therefore allowed themselves to doubt whether various masters and archangels actually possessed the light in their auras that they claimed to have.

Practically no spiritual person on this planet has consciously considered the idea that pure spiritually conscious beings could be in doubt about their belonging to the dimensions of Light or Dark. However, that really was the case for many beings in Earth's spiritual hinterland in the late 1990s. No one on the spiritual plane had the manifestation power to help them choose sides, so eventually they had to resort to asking for help from the earthly side, from some of the highly evolved people who at that time inhabited the planet. It was from here that the inspiration came to look even further, on a purely consciousness plane, into Earth's spiritual hinterland, to find a solution that could combine Light and Dark and other opposing energies into an even stronger energy constellation than we had ever previously been acquainted with here on Earth.

This is how the Shamballah force actually made its début several years before it was really supposed to.

THE SHAMBALLAH FORCE

It was not the Shamballah force's intention to destroy all of the Earth's old spiritual energy structure straight away. Its principal desire was to take control of the energy troops in the Hierarchy and prepare them for the influx of the New Time energy. Unfortunately, not all of the high-frequency energies in the Hierarchy were equally adept at mastering the influx of the new energy to Earth, which is why several conflicting messages were received by sensitive people on Earth during the transition period. This can happen no matter how evolved people and souls are.

The Shamballah force has always existed as both a supreme commander and yet also a very basic part of Earth's spiritual hinterland and the Planet's Internal Control, which reports back to all the planets in our solar system. This is because Earth is the common developmental planet for both of them.

On a soul level, we humans were not particularly aware of this energy's existence because of the various veils which appeared to cover it. If the most high-frequency human beings on Earth had been able to express the Shamballah energy through their personalities on a soul level, other, not so spiritually evolved people, might be afraid of these new and alien consciousness dimensions.

Therefore, it was only possible for relatively few very spiritually conscious people on Earth to make contact with the Shamballah force in a timely manner and this was only because they had 'prematurely' had their soul energy bodies lost in their auras which is why they appeared to be pure spirit to those above them. However, until AuraTransformation™, these people found it very difficult to materialise this energy on Earth in a concrete and constructive way. This treatment method creates the link between body and spirit, in the best possible way.

There have always been those who are first into the fray regarding new initiatives and concepts – those who probably have all the good ideas – and these people have apparently been chosen as pure channels for the spiritual dimension, so that global earthly consciousness can be prepared in good time for something new. The fact is that it would be most unhelpful if the entire population of Earth blacked out at the same time because of a particular new circumstance or energy state. This is precisely why we need precursors to pave the way for others.

We need people to fertilise new ideas and to carry things

through; people who have gradually been strengthened through spiritual preparation and are capable of taking the strain and dealing with any resistance from the surrounding world when information needs to be made public.

The time has now come to present some of the opportunities that come with the Shamballah force and from which we as humans on Earth can greatly benefit in our lives here.

Over the last 30 years, the Shamballah force has been working to store so much spiritual insight and knowledge in the Earth's aura that it has become possible for we humans to be able to consciously draw on this knowledge, if our personal consciousness is tuned in to it, as it can be after an AuraTransformation™. These days, people no longer need to move to the edge of insanity to be geniuses. We can keep our Earth connection intact throughout, regardless of whether we want to work very consciously with the spiritual development of Earth's hinterland, or whether we want to become the new Einstein. In the Shamballah force, there is room for both living in the spirit and living in matter, which is why everything needed for modern life is contained within it.

How we choose to spend our time on Earth, however, is a matter of personal responsibility. The only thing that is required to create space in the consciousness of we humans, so that the Shamballah force can have room to operate fully, is that we have the will and the desire in us to seek balance in our lives. We can then use will to decide which actions to take in order to support the consciousness work in the best possible way. You can do this by having an AuraTransformation™ which is a permanent change of consciousness, on all levels. Without an AuraTransformation™ it can be easy enough at the level of thought in our consciousness but things will not manifest as fully as they could when you do have one.

THE STRUCTURE OF
THE SHAMBALLAH FORCE

SPIRIT ENERGY IN SHAMBALLAH

The Shamballah force is the centre of DIVINE WILL–POWER, an all-embracing universal energy that is in everything and relates to all places. This energy is not only reserved for Earth and the planets in our solar system and their spiritual development. It is omnipresent.

The Shamballah energy is far more boundless and formless than the structure of the Hierarchy and energy-wise, we can equate the Hierarchy and the old soul energy with the first seven energy rays that have the 8th ray as a unifying factor containing the aggregate energy of the first seven rays within it.

The 8th ray thus contains the overview and the sum total of all previously established consciousness and energy knowledge, this ray appears outwardly to be the feminine, boundary-setting and will-governing part of the consciousness of the New Time.

The rays from the 9th to the 11th ray equate to the magnetic, masculine and action part of the New Time energy, which contains the energy for the dissemination of the message about the essence of the New Time energy. The essence of the New Time energy is, as mentioned, a balance between every type of energy. It is mediated particularly clearly through the 12th ray, which in turn is the unifying factor for the 9th to the 11th rays.

It is therefore no surprise that there have not previously been any specific masters and archangels associated with these energy rays, as everyone, in fact, works together in every possible direction.

However, if we combine the 8th and 12th rays, the energy of

the 13th ray emerges, which is the sum of all the energy rays together. This is the source of the energy of the Shamballah force in relation to the totality of the energy work carried out here on Planet Earth.

At the same time, the 13th ray is what is called a karma-free zone because there is no soul energy in it. The energy of the 13th ray was first and definitively opened up when the Hierarchy let go of its original control of Earth's spiritual hinterland, in February 2001.

The 13th ray is also the meeting point for will and action, which, as previously mentioned, belong to the 8th and 12th rays respectively. That is why it is logical that every child born today with the New Time energy already 'installed' comes from this energy.

Quite simply, New Time children are 13th ray children. Many adults also belong to this energy ray, which can become visible following an AuraTransformation™ when their full spirit potential has unfolded. 13th ray people in fact have no blockages in their spirit energy, as they are fully tuned in and have the ability to live and thrive in the New Time energy. These people have therefore often felt misunderstood by those around them in the old energy and have had a feeling of having been in an invisible straitjacket. This sensation disappears completely when they have an AuraTransformation™ because it allows them to release the old, restricting energy bodies in the aura.

Regarding the transition from the Hierarchy to the Shamballah force, all masters, archangels and others have had their old soul energy records deleted, which is why they all appear to be karma-free, which indeed they must have been already, otherwise they would never have been able to attain the status of masters and archangels in the Hierarchy!

Masters and archangels are just souls who, thanks to a major prolonged effort on the consciousness front and on behalf of the Whole, have earned the right to change over to pure spirit energy so that they could work closest to *God* at the zenith of the Hierarchy. They have always had contact with the Shamballah force, since it is from there, after being 'appointed' as masters and archangels, that they have drawn their extraordinary spiritual resources to assist the Whole even more than before, therefore greatly benefitting planet Earth.

In truth, the masters and archangels who have been given the task of working with Earth from within Hierarchy, have not had it easy, as they have had to reduce their great spiritual consciousnesses into a much more compact form, so that they could appear to have soul energy and therefore be able to be in contact with those people on Earth who were sensitive enough to detect the signals from the spiritual world. If they had just appeared with pure spirit energy, the inhabitants of Earth would perhaps have feared that they were aliens or creatures from outer space. So we can see that many things had to be taken into account from above in order to make contact with the very low consciousness capacity of people on Earth.

In other dimensions and worlds, Shamballah people – the masters and archangels and others – reveal their energies, as required, in completely different combinations and in multidimensional frequencies. In relation to Earth, however, they appear as bearers of either feminine or masculine energy, meaning spiritual inflow and physical outflow (or action), so they are a "match" for the overall energy structure of the planet. There is always balance in and around the Shamballah force, in the sense that opposing energies are always sent out simultaneously, in the form of say, light and dark to work on the very same tasks out in the different universes.

The Shamballah force is thus inhabited by masters who are extremely highly evolved, knowledgeable spirit beings, with a will made of the strongest substance in the universe - faith.

In addition, the Shamballah force is inhabited by the ancient archangels, who in relation to Earth, have had extremely powerful life experiences. They also have profound knowledge about both physical and spiritual contexts, with an emphasis on the latter.

Solar angels, who represent a real contrast to both the physical and the spiritual maturity of the archangels, are a group of younger and very energy-rich and luminous angels who, with their power and radiance, could dazzle and blind all around them if that is what they decided to use their power for. Also, they could reduce both their own and others' auras to ashes in record time. This is why many solar angels have very consciously been sent to Earth in the last thirty years, because on the Shamballah force's side, there has been a need to burn holes through people's auras in order to open their eyes relatively quickly to the necessity of integrating the New Time energy on Planet Earth.

Solar angels most often intervene in situations that require an extremely high light frequency to burn away old, useless energy in a relatively short space of time. They are clearly worth getting to know, if you can stand the heat.

All Shamballah people are, despite the overall balance within the Divine Unity, equipped with their spirit mass from which the Earth-related soul energy has been removed.

Soul energy has a very limited and somewhat localised perspective whereas spirit mass can be present and have several different aspects in widely differing parts of all the universes simultaneously. The scope is just not the same. However, spirit mass will always need to comply with the conditions of incarnation. So, no matter how spiritually conscious your original Shamballah spirit mass may be (if that is where you are from), as a human being on Earth, you will always need food, water, sleep, warmth and maybe sex in order to be able to exist, thrive and survive.

It was not particularly difficult for the Hierarchy's 'Commander-in-Chief' and the new spirit energies from Shamballah to work together when the influx of the New Time energy finally became a reality on Earth because, all of the Hierarchy's masters and archangels basically come from Shamballah.

Many of them even originated from the same spirit mass, which made it possible for them, on Shamballah's behalf, to take care of certain universal balancing tasks while acting as spiritual guides at the soul level for Earth. The masters and archangels emitting the highest frequencies have simply modified their frequency in order to adapt to the energy state of consciousness they might be expected to represent at any given moment down below on Earth.

The souls further down in the Hierarchy have not all been equally appreciative of the Shamballah force's influx of new, magnetic and boundless energy to Earth. They have found it difficult to adjust to the new *freedom-with-responsibility* consciousness, where you must set your personal limits regarding what you will offer yourself and others and what you think others may offer to you. They have therefore worked against the flow of energy in a major way, creating a great deal of resistance, especially on the subconscious level, which has often meant that the less evolved people are not able to succeed in life situations on Earth as they have been unable to understand why things keep going wrong for them.

These less evolved people, whose consciousness on the spiritual plane was further down in the Hierarchy, have thus often become victims to common consciousness control in the intermediate layers of the Hierarchy, where they have been encouraged, perhaps 'unconsciously', to be in conflict with those around them who have been even more spiritually conscious than themselves, meaning that the overall development on Earth would be stymied. However, now that the New Time conscious-ness has once and for all got its foot in the door of the earthly context, nothing can stop it.

SHAMBALLAH ON EARTH

On the earthly plane, those souls in the Hierarchy who have not yet had an AuraTransformation™ and the spirit beings from Shamballah, deal with the world in very different ways. They often come into conflict because of differences of opinion and irreconcilable ways of working. The Hierarchy's souls always follow the same rhythm in daily life and Shamballah people do not. However, this obstacle is removed immediately following an AuraTransformation™, as soul people will adapt and will be fully able to master the influx of the New Time energy.

The Hierarchy's souls need concentration and time for contem-plation. They want peace and quiet around them and to a great extent, they accept external authority in the physical world in the form of people with more important titles, more theoretical knowledge or more practical experience than themselves. They adhere to the model of the Hierarchy's spiritual energy struc-ture, where it is necessary to show humility in relation to more highly-evolved souls than one's own.

Shamballah people on the other hand, are used to circulating amongst others on all levels, high or low in the spiritual dimen-sion, where people with very different levels of consciousness and with the same interests but with very different approaches to things, take turns in taking the lead in certain circumstances, depending on which particular frequency is required. Here, there are no set rules or routines for the implementation of a specific project. On the one hand, Shamballah people may lack obedience to authority. On the other, they have a dynamism that can take them far and ensure that they achieve a great deal in a short space of time. As a rule, they are always ready to take on new, exciting challenges, if it feels good.

Everything is flexible, with space for new and different options and Shamballah people are always receptive to new knowledge, as long as it doesn't have to be learned in the old-fashioned way. Things should preferably be uncomplicated and proceed in a relatively effortless way. Even though they prefer to seek simple solutions in life, many, many thoughts stream through their heads every day that might sound very complicated if they were to try to explain them to others.

Shamballah people have well-developed intuition and will usually have an answer for everything quite quickly, either by listening to that intuition or by consulting others. When they act as a conduit for knowledge from the spiritual dimension, they do not get messages dictated by a spiritual guide as was customary in the Hierarchy. Instead, they just know things for themselves, since they are, quite simply, one of the spirit beings that people on Earth and souls in the Hierarchy used to consult.

The difference between now and then, in the implementation of spiritual energy on Earth, consists in people now being helped right down to the very matter of the planet on which they live their earthly lives. It is like when overseas aid volunteers are sent out to crisis- stricken areas with high levels of poverty, consciousness assistance has now been shifted down locally to Earth. This is due to increasing numbers of children being born with the new strong energy influx within them.

In the past, residents of Planet Earth either had to consult earthly gurus and priests, or guides on the spiritual plane. Sometimes, between their earthly incarnations, they had to go on "study trips" to foreign places out in the universes to learn new things. They then had to extend these new energy states to life here on

Earth.

Due to many souls taking time out from the physical plane in order to receive teaching on the spiritual plane in between lives and therefore slowing things down considerably in terms of Earth's development, it became imperative for the new energy influx from Shamballah to speed things up.

WHO HAS KARMA AND WHO DOES NOT?

Imagine a lot of spiritually conscious people who know nothing about the content of this book being told that they have no karma, that it had been settled long ago and that they were actually spending their time on Earth just to help to lift the planet into a higher and more luminous frequency in cooperation with everyone else. How would this affect their outlook on life? Suddenly, they would be as free as birds with zero spiritual debt. Think of the relief but perhaps also of the frustration of knowing that life can still be painful. Even if the wagging forefinger of the Law of Karma is no longer constantly reminding that you have to pay for the sins of your past, life can still hurt.

The Hierarchy has always been built around the concept of karma but the Shamballah force, due to its lack of hierarchical structure, knows nothing of that concept.

Shamballah, with its inner core of pure knowledge, stasis and feminine energy and its outer shell of adaptive, mobile masculine energy, is a karma-free zone, in that all souls when entering into it have relinquished all their previous human-related data and therefore relinquished their person-related soul energy. Karma is behind them and from then on, with the totality of their consciousness, they are part of the new mediating energy which Shamballah represents on Earth. By directly linking the higher mental energy, (or spirit body) and the physical body to a new balance body, which acts as intermediary, all the data that was previously stored on the astral plane in human auras is deleted, so that any karma you may have had is released for good.

The Shamballah energy can always find its bearings in the lower energy bodies of the aura but the lower energies are not able to find their way around on the spirit plane where the Shamballah energy is based. Therefore, a cooperation of equals cannot take place since the Shamballah energy is forever free whereas the astral energy, as far as earthly humans are concerned, is very limited by its karma and by the structure that previously characterised Earth's spiritual hinterland.

People who still have lower energy bodies in the aura will still need to seek spiritual guidance from other people with greater spiritual insight than them to avoid various physical karma problems. Shamballah people are making their energy available for this in the period to come, until all soul energy has left the Earth's spiritual sphere forever, which will happen within the foreseeable future.

We can see that many Shamballah people are born into more or less problematic conditions in their earthly lives, where they are surrounded by the old lower energy bodies in the aura just like everyone else. This is because, due to their frequently hidden energy work on Earth, they have, in the long term, found it easier to transform the bad stuff from the inside out rather than vice versa.

Just like the primitive societies of the past on Earth, many inhabitants of this planet still do not voluntarily seek spiritual assistance in their community, since they have no idea of why they should. The fact is that many people just don't know how far they have yet to go in their spiritual development and maybe do not even really care, as long as there is food on the table.

For a long time, the new high-frequency Shamballah energy has therefore been forced to sneak in through the back door by allowing many of its highly evolved spirit beings to be born into families with an extremely low spiritual consciousness. To the outside world it may have seemed as if these beings were just as low in consciousness as their low-frequency families. However, they were not like that on the inside. Thus, people may well be born karma-free, even if they live in squalid conditions and are not conversant with the 'correct' spiritual terms when they talk about life. Consciousness should always be sought behind the veil, not in front of it, as our bodies are just the shell into which we have chosen to be born in each incarnation.

In the years to come, far more Shamballah people will become visible, which is necessary if Earth's powerful development programme is to continue. The group dynamics which occur when many people with the same spiritual source come together, will help to shape the new world order, in which it will no longer be that a few people will pave the way on behalf of the Whole but instead everyone will take their turn for the benefit of both themselves and the Whole. If they do not do this, they will be allocated neither energy nor material resources. Further on in the future, economic poverty will thus be an expression of spiritual poverty, just as economic prosperity will follow the spiritually enriched people on Earth, those who have the best overall spiritual perspective on life. These people will not find it difficult to share their human and financial resources with other less fortunate people who also have the potential for spiritual development and earthly growth.

In the future, thanks to the end of karma, there will be much quicker manifestation in relation to every good or bad thought and action, which is why the justice principle will finally have found its legitimate place on Planet Earth.

If you should wish to keep your old karma – appropriate or inappropriate – you cannot hope for a quick, straightforward resolution of any present problems as the karma backlog will get in the way!

If, on the other hand, you choose the new aura with its much faster manifestation possibilities, you can always choose to hold on to the good things in life from before the AuraTransformation™. There are, of course, very few people who voluntarily want to let their old bad karma into their lives.

THE NEW TIME ENERGY

AURATRANSFORMATION™

In order to be a pure, optimal source that mediates the omnipresent Shamballah energy, some simplifications, in our energy systems and in our auras, have to be brought about.

The aura has to be changed fairly powerfully for it to be possible to integrate the masculine and feminine energies in a harmonious way in, so that balance can exist between the overall spiritual inflow and the continued physical outflow and action in life.

When it comes to integrating the new aura structure, we no longer need our etheric bodies, which serve to protect the physical body. This energy body is in fact far too vulnerable in relation to the new and very high-energy frequencies that are becoming the norm on Earth. In the future, very sensitive people will simply become physically ill or very mentally disturbed if they are not receptive to the New Time energy accessed through an AuraTransformation™.

For extremely down-to-earth people, it is perhaps not so much their minds that will be affected but rather their physical condition, in the form of illnesses such as allergies.

Since the concept of karma lies totally outside Shamballah's framework, in the future humans will also not need their astral bodies, where all old, current and future records about their lives are stored.

The people who originally come from Shamballah and who have already had a long life down here on Planet Earth, ignorant of their spiritual status, at least on an everyday consciousness level, have obviously all been equipped with an astral body, like those around them who were perhaps less highly-evolved. This was so they would not stand out from the crowd prematurely.

There are maybe just a few astrally clairvoyant people who have so far registered that Shamballah people's astral bodies are empty of information about the future. Clairvoyants have therefore been tricked into seeing things to keep the Shamballah people busy until they can be fully understood. In this way, 'the very quick ones' have been held back until other earthly souls have been ready to administer the New Time energy and make a consciousness shift at about the same time.

Shamballah people have never really needed to receive help from others, not even while still in their old soul-based auras. They have not needed to get advice and guidance from alternative practitioners who draw their spiritual information from the astral plane in the aura. However, given the way things have been on Earth, Shamballah people's spiritual ignorance on the earthly plane - but definitely not behind the scenes - has been the only way to spread a little light in the world – even in the alternative treatment world.

In the past and even now, when a Shamballah person visits an astral practitioner, huge amounts of energy are transferred from client to practitioner. This has helped the practitioner to open up even more to the influx of the pure new Shamballah energy.

The subsequent fatigue of the practitioner may well be caused by the energy refill that has taken place as if you are a pure channel for the highest energy, clients cannot take energy from the practitioner. Shamballah people do not in fact use their personal resources to treat people but rather they use their pure mediating ability. In this way, as practitioners, they set their own personalities to one side – the most difficult art to master for many practitioners. Many practitioners like to find confirmation of themselves in the energy, rather than accepting the things that they, as spiritual mediators, can pass on to the client.

There is no need for the lower mental body in the new aura, since this is where human logic and morality resides; factors which are based solely on physical observations and reasoning and which don't leave much room for the influx of spiritual intuition.

From now on, we will instead need qualities such as ethics and the capacity for overview, as well as a feel for the connection of things on all planes. This will enable us to master situations where both the mental and the emotional elements are involved. The lower mental body is unable to deal with the intensity of feelings.

****

Instead of having the old lower energy bodies in the aura, we humans need to be equipped with a magnetic and strongly protective balancing body and an updated aura structure which makes it possible to connect the higher mental body, which represents the pure spirit energy of human beings, with the physical body. This means that the path from thought to action becomes shorter. In this way, it will be possible to constantly remain grounded when doing any energy work, no matter how far you go up into the atmosphere. You will either be connected directly to the Shamballah energy as the spiritual guide you have always been and will therefore always be for others on the everyday consciousness plane, or else you will be directly connected to the overall force, so you can now receive intuitive guidance directly from there, without needing spiritual guides along the way.

As we have seen, the balance body and new updated aura structure create a direct connection between the spiritual and the physical elements. It is indeed possible to connect this permanently to your aura, if the three old lower energy bodies are released beforehand. Otherwise, an AuraTransformation™ cannot take place, as it would be impossible for the client to maintain the new state of the energy around the body if the old hierarchical structure were still in place.

Having an AuraTransformation™ may sound simple but only a trained practitioner can master the new, powerful, balance-oriented Shamballah influx sufficiently well that the process can be carried out in a responsible way. These practitioners are called Aura Mediators.

Removing the old energy bodies is not particularly difficult. In fact, clients often turn up for an AuraTransformation™ without the old energy bodies in the aura, feeling invisible to the outside world, which indeed they are. Those around them are often unable to relate to people who consist of pure spirit energy. If this spirit energy has not been aligned with the physical body through a balancing body, the spirit energy will take up too much space in consciousness. If you are unaware of this, you may well wonder why you are totally invisible!

Some of these clients may have been experiencing brief moments of balance but it requires too much energy to continue to try to manage the energy in this way. An AuraTransformation™ will do just that and in a very short space of time.

One thing that may surprise many people is, that after an AuraTransformation™, it is not always possible for astrally clairvoyant people to see that there has been a change in a person's aura and consciousness. This is because, as mentioned earlier, people with the old lower consciousness aren't always able to find their way further out in consciousness, whereas spiritually clairvoyant people can always get their bearings within the system.

The new balance body makes it possible for people to adapt their personal energy very quickly so that they can respond appropriately to both their own needs and the needs of others.

The magnetic quality of the energy body makes it possible to detect various signals and needs, both from within yourself as well as from the outside world. Since the energy body also acts as a permanent protective membrane, you will be able to adapt your energy appropriately and protect yourself in all areas of life. This means that you will stop always putting others before yourself.

The 'automatic pilot', that is to say the new balance body and updated aura structure, operate in many cases as a 'saviour' for we humans, making us react intuitively in emergency situations meaning that often, without even knowing it, we say the best things we could possibly say completely spontaneously! Lengthy preparation can often prove to be a waste of time once we are equipped with the balance body in the new aura. It is not that we become like puppets being controlled by a hidden hand from above – we are just able to adapt very quickly.

In the Indigo aura - the first updated version of the new spiritual type of aura structure that appeared in its pure form in 1995 - the balance body basically consists of a very deep blue-violet (indigo coloured) energy with many different coloured flecks in it which depending on mood and state of mind, can find a place anywhere in the aura to intensify things. So if you are very happy, your aura might appear as pure orange or golden and so on.

Generally speaking, the deep blue colour in the Indigo balance body relates to the channelling energy that works in a strong boundary-setting and facilitating manner on the physical plane. The violet colour relates to the transformative and spiritually clairvoyant energy that can simultaneously get things moving and make it easy to adapt. It is the combination of these two energies/colours that make it possible for you to be able to pick up other people's conscious or unconscious thoughts about you, while the energy makes it possible for you to either open or close your energy system to these thoughts if they are too distracting. You therefore have control over your own consciousness, and what you decide to fill it with, which is essential if you wish to work consciously on your personal development.

In the Crystal aura structure - an updated and lighter version of the Indigo aura that is fully developed in all newborn children's aura since 2009 and onwards - you find the same characteristics as in the Indigo aura. However, the big difference is that people with a Crystal aura also have crystallized body energy and are therefore pure cosmic fountains. They are completely self-contained systems in which other people can mirror themselves but cannot draw energy from. Under normal conditions they are capable of fully recharging their systems, providing they are in a quiet and balanced environment.

So far, it has been impossible to destroy the magnetic part of the balance body and updated aura structure when the balance body is permanently attached to the physical body. The protective part of the balance body, on the other hand, can be weakened if that is what the person decides. However, in the long run this might lead to physical and mental disturbances. Fortunately, most imbalances can quickly be corrected with an additional balancing session.

BALANCING

By letting go of the old lower energy bodies in the aura in order to allow the integration of the new balance body in the Indigo and Crystal auras, we simultaneously change our chakra structure. From seven chakras, we move to three in the Indigo aura and then to one in the Crystal aura. On the other hand, these three chakras and one chakra respectively contain the exact same energies as the previous seven chakras did, although they are far more concentrated in some much stronger energy constellations.

The three remaining chakras in the Indigo aura are *the heart*, *the hara chakra* and *the third eye*, or pineal chakra. The hara chakra and the third eye in the Indigo aura both correspond to the total heart energy that will eventually come to fill the entire aura in the Crystal aura. The heart energy and the aura will show with precision exactly where we humans are with our thoughts and our actions; just as far out into the atmosphere as we can imagine, and just as close to everyday life.

The heart is the balance point for we humans, where everything meets, or should meet, in harmony. As for the Shamballah energy, it is here that the feminine and the masculine energies unite into one strong, harmonious energy – an energy constellation with which all children were born, in a completely pure form - from 2009 onwards. Furthermore, any adult who has had an AuraTransformation™, will also have just one chakra left in their energy system when the Crystallisation process is complete.

The feminine energy is usually represented by the third eye with its spiritual insight and ability to see behind things whereas the masculine energy is represented by the hara chakra with its physical vigour and corresponding joy of living. The feminine, spiritual *inflow* and the masculine, physical *outflow* are every-thing that the human being's overall balance is aiming to master. In the Crystal energy, they are both represented in the heart chakra, which is the only thing we need to focus on balancing.

This balance between the masculine and feminine energies is necessary for us to become efficient and dynamic sources, down here on Earth, for the direct flow of the Shamballah energy to the planet. This state of balance cannot occur until the person has had his/her aura updated to either Indigo or Crystal as it is not possible to create this balance in the old energies of the

Hierarchy. In the Hierarchy, it was not unusual to see people with a predominance of either masculine or feminine energy, which meant that they would be categorised as either being down to earth or up in the air. This phenomenon will cease to exist under the auspices of the Shamballah, where the existence of both masculine and feminine elements in the aura is a prerequisite for achieving the overall balance required for a harmonious life.

Once the AuraTransformation™ and the subsequent balancing session have taken place, care must be taken when receiving healing from practitioners who have not had an AuraTransformation™. These practitioners may have difficulty getting their proper bearings and orienting themselves within the new energies, as they do not yet know of or understand these energies. They will therefore express themselves from their own levels of consciousness. This might very easily hold Shamballah people back, keeping them in old, outdated energy states.

If it is a matter of body-related treatments, such as reflexology or massage, it is not so vital that the practitioner is fully updated regarding the new energies, unless he or she works directly on the client's consciousness.

PROTECTION

Because of the new energy influx to Earth from Shamballah, it no longer suffices to ask for protection from *God*, as the concept of *God*, as mentioned earlier, corresponds to the highest authority in the old Hierarchy. We must instead move outside the Hierarchy with our consciousness – beyond the boundaries of the form and structure we have been functioning in up until now – and then out into totally new dimensions of consciousness to create optimal assistance and protection for our planet and for ourselves, when we work with energy and consciousness in our everyday lives.

We must move beyond everything we know and beyond all the frequencies that we think we have mastered up until now, to bring the greatest possible protection and most comprehensive healing energy down to Planet Earth and its inhabitants as we help to lift the frequency of Earth's energies.

All current and future energy work is now being carried out by the Shamballah people who inhabit the Earth but with a lot of help and support from the invisible spiritual hinterland, since we are living in a time when many spiritual people are incarnated as pure Shamballah people, often without knowing it.

If you want energy and protection from the highest cosmic source, you can invoke the *Original Source, the highest Divine source of love-intelligence*, or *the Prime Divine Creator*. Who exactly the highest energy source is, is of course, a matter of personal choice. Even if this energy has no name, it can be just as good as anything else.

If you recite this protection prayer out loud or quietly to yourself, you will be very safe:

I now envelop myself in a huge stream of Divine protective energy from the highest Divine source of love-intelligence for all time over all existing universes and non-universes and over the Shamballah force.

It might be complicated to ask for protection at this time as it is perhaps new for many people to handle such high energy frequencies on the physical plane. When you use many words, as well as your physical energy, to invoke the highest cosmic powers, you are helping to integrate even more of the high-frequency Shamballah energies on Earth. It must always be done in a way that feels appropriate to you.

HEALING

Everyone can heal if they so desire. Not everyone is able to feel energies and to know what is really happening during the healing process. However, if you wish to heal others, you can get good results by doing as follows:

First you pray (ask) for your own protection and that of your client by reciting the words mentioned in the previous chapter. After that, you can recite the following verse out loud or quietly to yourself, while putting your hands on the client and letting the energy flow through to him or her.

Always remember to end the session by washing your hands to release the client's personal energies, which do not, of course, have anything to do with you as a healer.

I pray (ask) to be a Divine source of the energy that 'X' needs directly from the highest Divine source of love-intelligence for all time over all universes and non-universes and over the Shamballah force so that 'X' can join in complete harmony with this highest Divine power.

I pray (ask) that the energy will come through very quickly, perfectly and in grace, so that 'X' can clearly feel and understand the energy and that it is to the benefit of and for the joy of 'X'.

You can replace 'X' with the name of the person, animal or anything else you wish to heal. Again, it is up to the individual which term he or she wants to use to describe the highest cosmic source.

It is most important, however, to always invoke energy directly from the highest place, as that way you avoid having to send the energy out to the right place in the client's consciousness.

The highest cosmic energy source, as we know, has insight and such incredible overview that it can easily assess where your client's needs are greatest, so that healing energy can go in that direction first. You may need, therefore, to divide the healing up into several sessions, if the highest cosmic source finds that this is what is most appropriate for the client.

With the influx of Shamballah energy to Earth, you will no longer need to invoke specific master or archangel energies as you did under the Hierarchy. This is simply because the energies in the Shamballah work together on every single level. You could therefore be in the position of not quite being able to recognise a specifically invoked energy when it finally comes through to you. This is because Shamballah, with its all-pervasive overview of consciousness knows much better than we do, in our day to day consciousness states, exactly what our energy requirements may be. Therefore, you should always seek energy directly from the top.

If you decide to seek help from a spiritually conscious person rather than consciously invoking energy directly from the highest place, you may find that you can ask a friend or a neighbour, provided that the person in question has had an AuraTransformation™. Many of the masters and archangels are currently incarnated on Earth as 'totally ordinary people' who could be your uncle or the woman working on the supermarket checkout. They are here to support the rapid acceleration of energy development on Earth. They work, like so many other Shamballah people at this time, directly from matter here on the Earth plane rather than only working behind the scenes in Earth's spiritual hinterland.

****

In Shamballah, everything is very straightforward, including working consciously with energy and magic. In fact, none of the old energy formulae from the Hierarchy can be used now, such as, for example, sending purifying white light to your surroundings to clean out the old unwanted energy states.

With the New Time energy, new energy methods have arrived. To learn more, you can read my book *"Balance on All Levels with the Crystal and Indigo Energies"*, which contains information on this subject.

"Balance on All Levels with the Crystal and Indigo Energies", is a practical, informative book which explains in detail the impact of AuraTransformation™ on human personality and daily life, masculine and feminine energies in their purest forms and other subjects which may well interest you.

STATUS

The energy status 1997 at the time of the initial release of this book, gave the impression that there was a long way to go before the Shamballah force could hope to be incorporated into earthly consciousness. Now, however, so many new children have been born with the New Time consciousness fully integrated into their auras from birth, that the global consciousness influx has had highly favourable conditions in which to flourish. If you look at the consciousness influx from a slightly more cynical point of view, you could also say that every day, more people who have carried the old time energy slip away from this Earth. Their old soul auras will be transformed on the spirit plane into a pure spiritual energy mass, which will no longer appear in the old, limited form. In the future, they will be born as pure Shamballah and 13th ray people – that is, if they are to be reborn on this Earth.

With each passing day, Earth is returning to its original energy source, which every human, consciously or unconsciously strives to get back to deep inside. When we are really close to this spiritual source, it suddenly occurs to us that we may need to let go of a lot of our original physical structure, which does not always feel comfortable. How can we exist without, for example, earthly input in the form of food and drink without risking death? Is there now a life for us in other dimensions of consciousness, or do we seriously risk being destroyed if we agree to let pure spirit energy into our earthly life? When you are pure spirit, you are dead, aren't you? Well, I would say yes, you are in a way - but now and for the time being, the intention is for us to function as pure spirit in a physical body on this Earth. This is a very real difference. When you have a physical body shell through which to express yourself, you also have the materialisation capacity within you to change the world, which the so-called 'dead' – or spirit beings, with no body shell – do not have. Who says that we shall slide back to nothing within the next thousand years or more? Who indeed truly knows? One thing is certain, however and that is that everything that was formerly defined as 'mystical' or 'elusive' on Earth will, in the future, become just as ordinary as what each of us perceives to be normal at this time in our lives.

Through the eyes of consciousness, Planet Earth quite frankly has a very long way to go before it 'risks' becoming a completely pure spiritual planet free of all matter.

****

My wish is that this small book will give you food for thought and that you may begin to look at life in a new, energy-updated' way. I hope that you will now get down, in earnest, to mastering your own life better than ever before.

My warmest regards

Anni Sennov

ABOUT ANNI SENNOV

Anni Sennov is the founder of AuraTransformation™ and of the Aura Mediator Courses™ which take place in different countries mainly in Europe.

She is a clairvoyant advisor, international lecturer and the author of more than 20 books about energy, consciousness and self-development, as well as New Time children and relation-ships, several of which have been translated from Danish into a number of languages.

Together with her husband Carsten Sennov, she is a partner in the publishing company Good Adventures Publishing and the management consulting and coaching company SennovPartners, where she is a consultant in the fields of personal development, energy and consciousness.

Anni and Carsten Sennov have developed the personality type indicator four element profile™ that consists of four main energies corresponding to the four elements of Fire, Water, Earth and Air, which are each present in everyone in a variety of combinations of balance and strength.

Multiple courses are offered on how to understand and integrate these elements both for private people as well as businesses.

Anni Sennov was born in Denmark in 1962 and originally began her career in the financial world. Since 1993 she has had her own practice of personal counselling and her great strength is her ability to clairvoyantly perceive multiple relevant circumstances pertaining to her clients' personality and consciousness.

Anni Sennov's work and books are mentioned in numerous magazines, newspapers and on radio and television in many countries.

You can connect to Anni Sennov's profile on Plaxo, Linkedin, Google+, Twitter and Facebook, where she has an English author profile:

facebook.com/pages/Anni-Sennov/141606735859411

You can subscribe to her English newsletter, become a member of her blog and see her travel schedule and event calendar at **www.annisennov.com**.

BOOKS BY ANNI SENNOV

BOOKS AVAILABLE IN ENGLISH:

Golden Age, Golden Earth

Balance on All Levels with the Crystal and Indigo Energies

The Crystal Human and the Crystallization Process Part I

The Crystal Human and the Crystallization Process Part II

Karma-free in the New Time

Spirit Mates - The New Time Relationship *(Co-author: Carsten Sennov)*

Get Your Power Back Now! *(Co-author: Carsten Sennov)*

The Little Energy Guide 1 *(Co-author: Carsten Sennov)*

Crystal Children, Indigo Children and Adults of the Future

Love, Sex and Attraction

See Anni Sennov's books in all languages at **www.annisennov.com**.